HEART SHAPED BRUISES

VEX LABOUCANE

Faet Thacker

Tellwell Talent
www.tellwell.ca

ISBN
978-0-2288-5341-1 (Hardcover)
978-0-2288-5342-8 (Paperback)
978-0-2288-5340-4 (eBook)

Dedicated to all who have lost their fight.

TABLE OF CONTENTS

HOPE
HEARTBREAK

(212)

How do people love one another?

Is there a cosmic predisposition
that draws the right people to the right places
at just the right time?

(160)

March into my life, let me introduce you to a new beat.

Everything you're used to, all the regular rhythms.

Forget what you've known, be prepared.
For your mind is about to be blown.

(64)

I know I don't seem like much
my flaws, a never-ending list.

I may not have much to give
all I have is my heart.

I hope that doesn't cost too much.

(193)

How does one fall in love?

Not with the idea of the person
or the things you see in them...
But to the actual person?

How do you see what they really are?
Can you love the things you see?

Even if they don't fit your idea
of what you wanted them to be?

What if you don't like
What it is...

      ...That you see.

(38)

Feelings rush to the surface.
Lust and excitement surge through.

Every molecule within my nervous system sparks a
light.

(34)

Moments like this—
I have to choose between showing you my soul
or attempting to hide it away.

My heart comes along so vulnerable, hurts easily.
This soul is already so weak
a shell of what it used to be.

(96)

They say being attracted to someone
is not just about their good parts
it's also about their pain.

So maybe my pain is attracted to your pain?

I've never known anyone whose pain matched mine.
An energy that is so dark, so deep.

I know each time we get closer
we risk opening up those wounds.

Do you think you're ready for me?

(32)

I always wanted a woman
who would spark my curiosity
during those times I'm by myself.

I longed for a lover
whose touch left me aching when I'm all alone.

Waiting for a day
when smut, and dirty films
would no longer cut it for me.

How did I not see you were right in front of me...

...Waiting all along?

(60)

Drum beats playing in my mind
got me wondering all the time.

Is there some sort of synchronicity
that connects us as one?

Does your heart match the rhythm in my head?

Do you sing the melody of my soul?
Could you be my remedy?

My perfectly matched melody?

(100)

Don't get too close.

Pushing back hard
I'll make you want to run.

A constant furious flame
burning brighter.
Raging so much hotter.

Unable to find a solution strong enough
to completely extinguish me.

Watch yourself.

I might just leave a scar.

(45)

I'm jumping over thoughts of you
I'm ducking my emotions too.

I've never felt something so true
I swear this came out of the blue.

How could I have known all along
you were the one I was waiting for?

Walked back into my life
told me I was yours from the start.

I had no idea you were right.
I am yours, but are you mine?

This topic, ignored all the time.
I will always think you're so damn fine.

(224)

Always been one to speak my mind.

Not thinking...
About the words...
As they come out...

Filling every awkward silence with nonsense...
Chatter chatter chatter.

Lately, I bite my tongue in quiet moments.
Not because what I have to say is unimportant
or unnecessary...

I've just found something worth holding back for.

The chance to hear her thoughts.
To feel the vibration of her words.

For those few rare moments
I will endure the silence.

Hearing those words pour from your lips.
I will hold my tongue.

For a chance to slip deep into your...

...Brain.

(119)

In love with someone who does not love me.

In a relationship with someone who does.

I will take what I can, for now, I guess...

(82)

Your aura surrounds me, yet I feel so alone.
I ache to be all yours.

Will it ever be...
...Just you and me?

(56)

Like the honey mustard
you put on absolutely everything...
You're a beautiful mix of so many flavours
converging into one.

I want you to be my forever-thang.

—Cheesy things I wish she would say to me.

(150)

My body aches for your touch
my heart desires yours.

Even when we're apart
I still feel you next to me.

Your love is all I've ever needed.

You've awoken inside of me
a deeper excitement than any I've ever felt.

(226.1)

Can she care for me?
Will she nurture my soul?
When I'm sick, would she make the right soup?
Coerce me into a warm bath?

I think she could be the one who I can rely on...

(232)

She is cool water
while I am burning fire.
Remaining grounded on earth
when I am off floating in space.

Our signs are so different
yet she balances me.
Four elements cumming together...

She ignites a flame within me unlike any other.
This flame burning inside hungers for growth.
Channelling that passion is necessary.

It burns so bright; I must be careful.

Risen from a pile of ashes and dust
A Phoenix reborn.

Looking and learning
with her by my side...

...I might become Majestic.

(187)

On days like today when the sun doesn't shine
I want to cuddle up in a blanket
with the one I love the most.

This is the worst part of a long-distance relationship.

If we were together
we could drink warm beverages.
Share sleepy kisses and fat doobies.
Enjoy a candlelit bath
watch movies by the dozen.

She's all I feel.
She's all I hear.

My whole body shakes when she whispers in my ear.
Everything...
                    ...Trembles...

        ...Under...

        ...Her...
            ...Touch.

(41)

Deep inside, I'm worried; I try to keep it buried.
Insecure because of a thing I can't change
a part of me that I do not have.

Will you leave me to seek that part?
Would you miss the feeling
of something I cannot give you?

My whole life I've attempted to cover this.
Failure to hide has left me vulnerable.
How can I give you everything?

...If I don't have a Dick?

(77)

One on one, two by two.
No matter the equation
the answer is always me and you.

Three times three, four plus four.
I will always love you
even if we're poor.

Five minus five, six divided by six.
I will always crave
our extremely passionate sex.

(194)

Her beauty shines through the screen.
All these picture messages steal my heart
even during this time we are apart.

Wondering to myself...

"Why am I so attracted to you?"

In these photographs I can see, you're so, so sad.

Don't get me wrong
your smile lights up my life.
But there's this fire I can see hiding behind your
eyes...

Slowly...
Smouldering...

In these moments, you flash your hopeless smile.

Desire to take you...
...Rough...

Hard-core fucking...

Making *hate* to you...

...Why do I WANT to hurt you?

You're the one who makes me feel better...

(42)

The craving I have to give you everything
leaves me afraid and wondering.
You've experienced things I cannot give.

Do you crave the easy, simplicity of a boner?
How easy to tell you've turned them on.
The quick slip out of pants and into you.

I cannot give this to you.
Your entire life, that simplicity is what you're used to.

How can I compare?
How can I compete?
I'm not even in the same league.

(210)

How do I let go of these things I know?
Even though you are with me now?

Nobody will get between us.
Only you matter to me.

I need you to show me that it's the same for you.

(31)

Why must I fall for such unreliable people?

I desire so much from the ones I love.
How could anybody be what I need in full...

Sure, you excite my sexuality like nobody ever has
but can you be there for me when I need you?

Will you sweep me off my feet?

Can you captivate my interest?

Intrigue me long enough?

Can you be every little thing I need you to be?

(184)

Waking up over and over.
Mostly bad dreams, sometimes good ones too.
Any movement or sound had me shot up out of bed.

I drank myself to sleep night after night.
That never left me rested.

Nothing could ever keep me asleep.
Now I sleep next to you peacefully
even when you get up to leave.

You always come back in to find me
still deeply, fully asleep.
I wake up completely rested.
More in love than ever before.

(181)

I watch as you walk into my office.

As if you belong here.
At home among the files
you saunter past me...

...Knowing damn well I'm picturing you on your
knees.

Nothing can be done about that.

Not until I've finished this sale...

I want to feel you so badly.
The anticipation is eating me alive.

Trying to remain calm
afraid I'll crack under the pressure.

With the rip of the debit slip
and a click of the locking door
I am in the clear.

I'm undressing myself, coming to find you...

Sitting there, half exposed
flashing your lingerie underneath.
Legs spread wide
you motion me forward.

Peeling my shirt over my head I lean in
kissing you deeply.

We could get in trouble for this.

I don't even care.

I need to feel myself inside of you.

This is what I live for.

(205)

Feeling insecure, my biggest weakness.
What we have burns so bright.
I know how we feel is oh, so real.

Tell me why do I desire to escape?
To run away and never, ever look back at the mess
I left.

I'm feeling trapped, most likely by you.

My long-term job has me dreaming...

Dreaming of all the vacations.
Chances to finally be irresponsible.

I miss feeling free.

(227)

The way her body moves subconsciously
reaching out, desperate to touch me.

When I join her in bed
our feet tangle in the sheets...

      ...My heart always skips a beat.

(234)

I love to feel her body against mine.
Her silky skin is always soothing to the touch.
She has the bluest eyes I have ever seen.

I could spend my days relaxing
inside that icy, yet refreshing gaze.

(192)

I yearn to feel you, waiting to hear your call.

Your hands, without even trying
leave a lasting impression.

Making me believe.

Maybe I could be beautiful...

(29)

Those icy blue eyes freeze me.
You rush through me, quick as a chill.

I feel you linger, even when you're not around.

Up and in my spine, like you've touched me.
Goosebumps tingle my skin.

I feel your hands pull back my hair.
I crave the taste of you on my lips.
I long for your silky body against mine.
I ache to hear you say my name.

You're so intoxicating, like the kiss of death.

...You take my breath away.

(81)

I'm confused.
Why am I feeling so blue?
I know what we have is special
between me and you.

Not together
but forever as one.
I feel your despair.
Your anger is...hot.

Far away yet the feeling remains the same.
You have become a part of me.

Changing the very structure of my DNA.

(40)

I don't know how to love you.

I want so much to just be me.
You've told me that's what you want too.

Telling me to "shake a leg," backpedalling when I try.
Like a child again, rejected...

Hiding parts of myself away.
Unwilling to expose the deepest reaches.

I guess it's for the best to keep this inside.

(200)

I've always tried to keep my promises.
Wouldn't make ones I couldn't keep.
Show up when I say I will, all that jazz.

Are you some sort of fucked up karma?
Promising me the world, leaving me disappointed.

You show up empty handed or not at all.
All the while my heart is breaking.

Feelings of not being good enough.
Emotions once forgotten, now my daily expression.

I haven't always been innocent.
I've broken hearts, told lies, constantly cheated.
The occasional stealing
expressing myself with violent acts.

Unable to dig deep enough to forgive or forget.

When you walked into my life, I thought I was ready.
It was finally my time to love
and be loved properly for once.

I got my shot at something beautiful.
So why is it, even though you say you love me
I am still not worthy of love, nor the effort?

I try and try to give.
I'm growing weary.
My attempt to go unseen.
Unreceived and unreciprocated.

How can I be worthy of your all?

(213)

What happens when you mess everything up with
"the one."

If I never find the right place
I'll for sure miss the right time.

Even then, could I still be the right one for you?

(12)

The words escape me; it seems you do too.
How can I explain why I feel so blue?

I know it's 'cause I like talking to you...
When I can't, it's, like, *"I dunno, what did I do?"*

'Cause the way I see it, you used to blow up my phone.
I thought it was cute and found it sweet.
It was something new...
...Until we had sex.

Seemed like a lot but maybe not enough.
How it was for me isn't always what's true.
I've got my brain all wrapped up with you.

I need to know; do you feel this too?

I wonder certain things all the time.
Every person who gets close to you.
Do they feel the fucking rhyme like I do?

Curiosity will kill the cat (once at bat)

You've got the charm, temptress, like seduction.
You can have everyone and anyone you'd like.

Am I really the only one? *(I can still taste the sambuca)*

(26)

Left to feel like dust, slowly collecting on a shelf.

Unaware of which direction to take
not knowing where to go.
Undesired and hopeless, feeling all alone.
I'm wondering why you left me here to die.

You tell me all the time how you want me.
How you want my rhyme.

You say you're in it for the long haul
yet I'm sitting here doubting you.

(204)

Your soft, erect little nipples call to me.
They scream for me.
Wanting inside my mouth
while my hands push both breasts closer together.

The feeling of your hands in my hair
pulling me, guiding me...
I know you like this control
so this time I'll let you have it.

Once I have the chance to take you, exactly perfect
that's when I'll have you how I want you.

I'll tie you up...

...All wet and begging.

I'll take control.

Someone doesn't like doing what she's told...

(13)

Sleep now or forever hold your peace.
The day will come when you lay your head
knowing all is well and all is right.

That feeling may never come.

For better or for worse, always by your side.
When we kiss, we say "I do."
Hand in hand, this moment so raw.

One eye open, I don't think we really meant to.

Poverty or wealth, supportive to the core
I desire to be your one true lover
I promise not to bore.

Excitement spinning down the drain.

Bank account is looking thin.
Make it stretch just one more time
our love could be tossed in the bin.

But yet we hope for more.

(61)

Blue roses, just because
Symbolic of your unattainable love.

Hung from the ceiling when you look up to the sky.

Left on the sidelines to dry.

(254.1)

I know you need distance, more so than I do.
How, don't you see I go crazy when you're not around?
Left to question myself, my sanity on the line.
Does it make you happy leaving me reckless?
How do you get off on my mental torture?

Why do I let you do this?

(242)

The effort is more one sided, no longer is it equal.
I've been lied to.

Every time you don't show up, I feel unimportant.
Not nearly good enough...

I'm watching our relationship plummet.

(27)

How do I hold back when I want to give you
everything?
How can I keep this to myself
when all you have to do is ask?

Where do you go when you go to think?

How can you hold back from me?

Why are you like this?

Questions I want to ask but won't.
Answers I'll never know.

Do I stand by while you rip my *fucking* heart
right out of my *fucking* chest?

Shred me to pieces, I don't even care.

(257)

Told me you loved this feeling, told me you cared.
Lie after lie is all it was.

Are you lying to me or to you?

(30)

Is this what you meant
when you said you needed space...?

Even though you're miles and miles away
you like to chill alone at your place?

Hour after hour, day after day
without a comment or a call.
Left to hang no word at all.

I wonder what exactly did I say?

Is it me that's far too needy?
Is it me that you do not desire as deeply?
I try to understand, and I try to stay calm.
My broken pieces scream at me.
"Listen close so you will hear the truth behind the lies."

I *so* want to believe you.

(207)

I still feel the love I felt under the tree
that summer we spent together.

How things have changed...

Mostly us.

That's how life goes; it forces you to grow.

I am pained by thoughts of how I left you.
Even more so tortured by the fact...

...That I still love her.

The girl who paid for my love.
This little thing who never smoked or got too drunk.
Someone who never did anything bad.
You were sweet, loving and oh so caring
always going out of your way for me.

Like I said, life forces us to grow.

The things I loved about her, no longer exist within
you.
If I don't feel like I used to
was this better off being a summer love?
Is this the real deal?

Or do I just need to open my eyes?

(1)

A Frankenstein of all my favourite people.
Take bits and traits from each one.
Stick them on you, adapt a personality.
Mimic a smile, copy a hairstyle.

Mashed parts and pieces
hardly recognizable.
Together swirling into a chasm
no longer identifiable.

I can't seem to shake
this "familiar feeling" stirring inside.

Do I recognize your soul? Or just the Monster I see?

A mystery right in front of me, marvelled by your
beauty.
Sensory nerve endings, firing within.

Won't you show me who you are?

(241)

My heart pains from a love not reciprocated.
Love may not even be the word.

You don't show—but you swore you felt it too.
Words echo with empty promises.

Unable to decipher what is sincere and what is fake.

Why must you be such a fucking flake?

White as snow.

Basic ass.

Narcissistic bisexual bish.

(58)

I have hope for our future, I often reflect upon the past.
All of our encounters...seven years this love has lasted.

I only hope the next decade will be a bigger...

....more explosive blast.

(39)

Taught to believe love is wrong.
Not the typical, soft type of love.
Anything that doesn't fit the norm.

Deep within myself, cravings
unlike anything I've known before.

I want to see her beg
on her knees, head to toe in sweat
sucking and licking as she's told.

Chains keep her how I like to see her
nameless, faceless.

Quick hookups covered in filth.
I want her to feel less than human.

Worthless and totally unlovable.

(69)

Your pale skin glowing in the thin night light.
Moon shining in through the blinds above your bed.
Through that big bay window.

...That big fucking Bay window...

Where I'd stash half empty cans
littering them with cigarette butts.
Each one enjoyed between *love-fucking-making.*
We always made love...

Forever feeling that moment
as real as ever and as present as today.
Your beauty astounding me
as intensely since *FOUR-fucking-ever.*

Like the first time I *saw* you.
How your lips curved, and your eyes twinkled...
Moments persevered in my mind.

I knew then, as I know now...
 ...that my love for you is eternal.

The passion inside aflame for you...

...Constantly *fucking* screaming
 (her name).

Every nerve in my body knows this bond will
withstand any qualms and any quirks.

Until *FIVE-fucking-ever.*

(16)

Who the fuck do you think you are?

Coming in here like you own me.
Bitch, you ain't get to touch this.

When the fuck you gonna leave me be?

(115)

Searching thoroughly.
Deep within the darkest crevice
that remains inside my mind.
A lonely space reserved for you.

I've found I miss you
suddenly I'm writing again.
Still, I'm spitting angry.

Discovering again each ounce of desire.
All of the passion our love ever held.

Reimagining all of the things:
Plush pink lips, the delicious flow of your hair
the soft melody of your voice
your sweet-sounding laughter.

I no longer see light
I can only see you.

Why am I trying to shut you out?

(236)

She is not the one who broke me.
She isn't like the one I left before.

Even when she did hit me, that was a "mistake."
A flash of trauma, slapped into her...
By some other man's...
...Unworthy*fucking*hands.

I know she won't hurt me again.
We both have seen how shitty it can be...
When it's not her and me.

2)

From the days in the park. Damn, we've come far.
Drinking screech and yielding to vices.
Damn, we've come so far.

Do you recall that time your sister told me to leave?
When you were too high to say goodbye?

I couldn't stand the thought of you not seeing me off.

From the days in alley
Damn, we've come far.
Pulling my strings, treating me like a king
Damn, we've come so far.

Dozens of drunken parties.
Messy cab rides home.
Desperate flings never mattered when I was always
at your 'Bec' and call.

I should have known then what I know now.

Heart filled with hope that I'd be your boo.
Mind soaked with despair, I came to you.
Turned away with a simple "no."
Tear stained years, I thought I'd lost you.

From the days apart
Damn, we've come far.
From the hurt and all the games
I cannot believe we have come this far.

(103)

Black on blue, like me and you.
Bruises on my soul, mistaken for hearts.

Signs of love all confused...

Random acts of violence.
Tear me down, rip open a new one.

...Just promise to kiss me to sleep.

(48)

Soup snakes.

The thing about soul mates is...

It doesn't mean you automatically get along.
The soul connection type of relationship
is just like every other relationship out there.
It takes work, understanding, patience, and kindness.

The thing about relationships and being in love...

It isn't easy, and it sure as hell isn't always kind.
However, through trial and error
you get one step closer to understanding.

It may seem pointless at times.
I know every trial as well as each error
can and *will* bring you together if you both try.

See, the thing about soul mates
who find each other maybe at the wrong time
or too soon, is that things go wrong.
Feelings get hurt, things get said that never
ever should have been said.

They often let go and walk away...
However...

The difference with soul mates that fail and give up
is they always feel them as a piece of their being.
You will forever hold a piece of your heart for them.

Regular relationships no matter how much love
you can always walk away.

S. Girl. I know, no matter where life takes us
how far away we drift
how many other lovers we take.
I will always know in my heart that you're the one.

I will forever feel your heart beating with mine.
Nobody will ever measure up to the feeling
of us being together.

I know I am hard to love
I know I make loving me a challenge.
Possibly even more difficult than any regular person.

I am no good at love
or expressing myself in a healthy manner.

I know this makes it tough.

However, you make me wanna try.
You make me wanna trial and error
until I run out of breath.
If I get that chance to trial and error with you
I would hope to go on breathing
for a very long time.

(216)

You are my home, away from home.
So why don't I feel safe anymore?

My soul lives within you, so what lives within me?
Deep inside calling to me, saying awful things.

Hurting me...

Is that you?
Or Is that still just me...?

(98)

Here I go again, same old cycle.
Exactly the same pattern.
Turn the dial, here I am again.

What you wanna say to me?
You have no game to play for me.
Play as you will, expect no gain.

I've come here, I've gotten so far...
...No stopping this.

(191)

Your silver tongue glistens now that my eyes are open.
Blindfolded and gagged describes my love for you.

No longer will I stay silent.
Time to open these eyes.

I will find my footing...

I can't kick this new habit.

(111)

When I think of my life, I see you.
Forever my soul's "wife."

Always by my side.
Without you, I would be a nightmare.

Decades of comfort, having you close by.
My heart would break were we to be apart.

Rest assured, my longest love
I'll follow you quickly, to the grave and thereafter.

(138)

We may not see eye to eye
clearly, we tend to butt heads.

It's been stated, I crave feeling special
wanting only your attention.

Starving for the warmth of your love
When the clock struck midnight
All I got was a measly text.
What I needed was a hug.

Aching for your touch.

Left to fall asleep.
Sad, cold, and all alone.

Happy fucking birthday to me...

This is what I deserve.
Nothing short of disappointment.

(35)

Stuck between two roads, unable to choose.
How does one make this choice?

How to determine the path less painful?
Challenges lie ahead.

Toxic heat within the sheets.
Friends have walked away.

How to decide?
Who can make this choice?

(14)

As the night starts to grow
it's more apparent now I know.

This isn't what I wanted.
You aren't what I wanted.

We lived in a fantasy for far too long.
We lived a lie for far too long.
Grown adrift, two worlds apart.

How could I have ever fucking considered
giving you this heart?

You would have dropped it
Mother-fucking lost it in the drainpipe.

You would have smoked it.
I bet you would have choked it
mother-fuck would have broken it.

When I hold her so close, I just lose it.
I can't help this feeling, thinking it's real.

You mother-fucking lost it.

BLOOD
TEARS

(47)

Isn't it tragic...

When something that could have been beautiful
dies before it ever blossoms?

Isn't there something poetic
about the tragedy of a failed flame
or a forgotten flower?

It will always be remembered
for what it could have been.

Not for what it actually was.

(217)

I know when I leave my heart will ache.

My lips will tremble...
Reminiscent of you.

I'll still feel how you kissed me.

I won't forget the days and nights
we were so lucky to have
nor the way your hands felt on me.

I'll crave the way you make me whimper
while everything inside me shakes.

(83)

S. girl, it's been one hell of a ride; I see us in the future.
You saw me for all my flaws.

I hope you accept *us* before my clock stops...

(190)

Growing up, I always acted a fool.
So, they called me one.

Jokes made about itchy noses
explained why I fell for you.

Only a fool would...

A match made in heaven
this girl with an itchy nose and me.
The biggest fool to ever lay eyes on you.

The first time I let it slide.
Fool me once, and I still love you.

Second time around, I decided to forgive.
Even though shit behaviour
is completely unacceptable.

Fool me three times and, baby
you're the real fool.

I would...
...Have done anything for you.

(231)

The word departure scattered all over the bus depot.
What does it mean to me?

Obviously, to leave is the first thing to come to mind.
Leaving behind a city you barely even knew
but grew to love more and more.

Now I'm home.
This familiar place, the faces, the buildings, the
roads...
I know them all. I know them well.

Why is it they no longer feel like I belong here?

(188)

I hope one day to wake up
realize why we had to break up.

We were supposed to grow together.
Instead, we grew apart.

How can two people in love
live inside one shared heart?

(93)

1994, the year you were conceived.
Your energy shifted this world so extremely.
Nothing has since been the same.

Your beauty is oh, so bright
gives everyone a hell of a fright.
Deep down, we all just want a piece.

Here we are...
Years after you waltzed out of your "birth giver."

The queen of my heart, you are.

Knowing you'd get away with it
you stabbed me in the back.
Left me to feel so blue.

You knew what you did.

Or, maybe you didn't even realize
every star in space finally had a purpose.

Contradiction since your first breath
a beauty but also a mess.
Perfection in all your flaws.

To look upon your gorgeous face
basking in the glory of being alive.
The world became significantly luckier
the day you graced this planet.

November 7, 1994, a day to be cherished every year.

Watching old shows, I'll laugh.
Listening to "our" songs, I'll dance.
Loudly and trashy
the way you like it.

Eat hearty meals similar to the ones you used to
make.
Rubbing my ears
thinking of your lips.

I will wait patiently until you love me.

Wow, I'm basically turning into a stalker.

(18)

Struck down with nowhere to go.
I'm left overwhelmed and undesired.

When I chose you
I thought I knew all the pain you had.

Without having been shown
how could I have known your heart was so cold?

Do I still love you? That would be so bold.
For me to give my heart over.

Let you fill the empty space.
        I need to run for cover.

How I love seeing you, in this isolated place.

To hand myself into the unknown.
The scariest thing I'll ever do.

Why must you be the absolute best bone?
I cannot stop loving you.

                Even now you've let me go.

(20)

Next time you call, will I answer the phone?
Mostly, I like to think no.

When you do, I only let it ring twice
before I inevitably kneel to your need.

I hear the whisky in your voice.
You're craving a slip between my thighs.

Failing to fight back the words...

"Come on over, I'm all alone."

(33)

I've resorted back to dirty films
Not even smut can cut it.

Unable to watch films featuring women
despite there being one I fiercely crave.

The men in the video? Nothing to be desired.

The passion is what gets me.
Love, sex, and burning, the beautiful act itself.

Your face bubbling up, into my mind's eye.
I push it back, fight with the thought of you.

It's impossible to cum...

How am I supposed to feel alive...

...When you've left me here alone to die?

(15)

Your voice on a loop.

"Overflow all over me, I want your full capacity."

Your words rush through me with such excitement.
I quiver under the weight of your voice
as it slams into me...

Do you remember the feeling of slamming into me?

How you would moan in ecstasy
with each push deeper inside?

(50)

Heteronormative Bisexual Bish.

I miss you, like my myocardium misses a beat.
Going into half of a heart attack.

You are not here
when I need you to be.
Like you're not at all queer...
I do not miss it at all.

I do not desire to skip a fucking single beat.
All I desire is regularity
unlike the only consistency you know.

How *not* to be there.

I FEAR THE DAY I MISS THE RHYTHM OF YOUR
HEART.

(17)

Fuck the blackness of your heart.
Fuck my lungs so filled with tar.
Fuck the coffee that we drank.
Fuck the way you smoke in my car.

I used to think the way we touched
meant more than just a lay.

I used to think the way we laughed
rumbled deeper than regular play.

Even though you hurt me
you told me we were meant to be.

You told me to let you go...

...I know I won't let go.

(112)

Irony always falls
each and every which way.

This love so intense
our hate is equally matched.

Both addicts
slaves to different vices.

The split between us
impartial to its core.

Inevitable is our life together
yet we remain unavailable to one another.

(59)

Since your name graced my lips...
Certain routine phrases
Coined sayings tossed around
have ever since changed meaning.

I've always been passionate
I will forever be intense.

You're the spark that lights my flame.
The fuel for my burning fire.

I would love for you to kindle me once again.

(91)

Every road in my life points towards love.

Your heart speaks to me
navigating me from within my bones.
Steering me through stormy weather.
I always make it home.

Street lamps shine in high hopes that one day
I might find you standing there
glimmering and shining
like the goddamn goddess you are.

I feel no matter how far we stray
the planets will align.
(If they have to)

For me to find you again.

(65)

I long to feel your touch, I ache to graze your lips.

...Just...
 Barely on mine.

Making me want for more with every breath.
To inhale the pure essence that is you.
A pleasure I wish for on a daily basis.

I know I've said it before
I'll share this desire once more.
If you honoured me with another chance...

...I'd fucking make sure to get it right.

(249)

Life as we knew it shattered as it shook.
A whirlwind of bad decisions.
Separated not only by days.
Wedged apart with grief and disdain.

(146)

You are my beginning...

Not what I want, you're what I need.
Obsession fogs my mind, thinking of you all the time.

Every night dreaming of us.
I can't stop wishing for things to have gone differently.

...You'll also be my end.

(113)

Left wondering where things went
oh so goddamn wrong...

Will I ever actually know?

(135)

Exposed and vulnerable, told you everything.
My deepest...
 My darkest...

Reassured me you'd be there.
Yet I'm still left facing them alone.

(211)

We got it all wrong.
Oh, this is just a mess.
How were we supposed to know?

It is always going to be, you and me.

68)

Thoughts of you haunt me
tormented by nightmares.

Day and night, it's all the same.

The way you ran your fingers in my hair.

Your scent filling my nostrils
clinging to my soul.

Missing the feeling of your lips kissing every inch.
Sighing deep moans into me.

My ears ache for your breath.
My tears fall wishing for you to catch them
kiss them away.

Reliving every moment we spent together.
Dreaming up our fictitious future.

Insomniac.

(66)

Thoughts of you flood in while I'm alone.
I'm drowning, not knowing up from down.
This black abyss embracing me.
Holding me tight, pulling me deeper.

Thinking of you only seems to sink me.

(173)

Left to my own devices, I always run.
Commitment is too scary.
Back around, no doubt I'll stray.

Yearning for you, a whole new craving.

Destined to never get...

...This fix...

...Has me dying.

(159)

Perhaps I shall always regret
never having a meal with you.

Well, not one in my apartment, anyways.

With my decor and my furniture.
Just once, to retain the imprint of our love.

We would share the one clean plate I have.
Joke about the twice reheated coffee.
Take turns feeding one another.

Letting fingers linger on lips... *ha.*
Feeling the tension build with each graze.

Now spread out across my messy sheets...

Smoke in one hand
looking up at me.
Your tank top askew
my boxers from before.

Your hair is a mess, that radiant smile of yours and...

....You're...
...Glowing.

Momentarily, I'm brought back to reality.

Piecing together beautiful moments.

...from us having fun at your place.
Stitched into cut scenes at my place.

Uhh... In case you didn't know
you fit here... Perfectly.

Luckily for me, I studied every inch of you.

Again, my mind begins to wander
to those slender, bony
pale white as the bones themselves...
..Fingers.

They're picking up my favourite spoon
tracing the etching along the handle.

I know you'd ask me about it.

I tell you of my great grandma.
How it's been in my life as long as I have.

I'm watching as you put the spoon up to your...
..Thin...
..Yet luscious, ever so kissable pink lips.

You look at me, and your eyes are breathtaking...

I can feel my heartbeat rising already.
I know, this isn't a "healthy" coping mechanism

...I just don't know...
...How...
...Or, What else...

...To do.

(171)

Stumbling towards you
I'm mumbling some nonsense.

Hard to understand
you're unable to make it out.

Trying so desperately to decode my message.

When all I said was

"I love you."

(94)

One thing I know for sure
is just how much I hate myself.
This self-loathing knows no bounds.

It's no wonder
you're constantly unimpressed by the pity party.

Emotional rollercoasters
taking me to various places
where no one could ever understand.

I've accepted who I am.
Pieces of me cannot change
they will soon devour me in rot.

Rot away day by day
fermenting in the wallow.
Black abyss that is my mind.

A constant state never knowing.
Nor caring, nor loving.

Always, always leaving.

(101)

Destined never to get close to anyone ever again.
A curse has been cast over me.
Eternity spent with a spell affecting my life.

Dark rain clouds
constantly hovering.
Nothing left now but a mess.

This heart, barely beating.

A hopeless romantic
Now slowly freezing
turning to ice.

Always alone, isn't that tragic.

(4)

Thinking back...
It feels like a lifetime ago.

We fell in love.
Waking up at the crack of dawn.
Those days are so far gone.

The person I once was
is long forgotten.
Buried deep inside
covered in dust.

Time to wake up to a fresh start.

Let me shake off the rust.

(49)

The fake (all too real) tinder profile:

I am a serial monogamist, commitment-phobe.
Drawn to settling down.
Running to someone else when things get too real.

I am a sado-masochist, Gemini-Aries.
With a fetish for ears and a desire to cause chaos.

I value those who are loyal to me
without the feeling of loyalty to anyone but myself.
Bound to muck up the best things.

420-friendly, pot head.
Love-hate relationship with booze.
Man-hating, gold-star lesbian.

(106)

Night after night
feeling like an animal.
Ready to take flight.

They flock to me by the dozen.
Taking piece by piece.
Never caring to know how frozen my heart really is.

I learn something new every day.
The name of whomever I wake up to.

The beast inside is satisfied...

...At least for today.

(137)

I once asked you to hold me while my mind taunted me.

You left me feeling hopeless
despite saying you wanted to be there.

I'm left haunted, with no one in sight.

(155)

Isolating within my own self.

Keeping the blinds down
door locked.
Lights off
sitting within my own dark thoughts.

Not a soul allowed in
nobody to judge me.
Left alone to drown.

Taken under by waves of despair.
Swallowed alive by sadness.

Soon the rage will surface.
A false lifeboat
one that will only push me deeper...

...Into the depth of my own demise.

(248)

I'm never alone, a darkness follows.
Forever creeping...
Not even sleeping.

This disease for sure will be the death of me.

(67)

Centuries spent seeking the light
lost in shadows for so long.

Coldness creeping in
chilled to the bones.

Reminding me the task at hand.

Search for brightness
looking to the warmth.

I will be back to you one day.

(72)

Every time I pick up a book
Brand new and shiny
or old, and a lil bit dusty.

I take a moment to really just look.

I wonder if she did the same
alone on that rainy day in her reading nook.

Those autumn afternoons when it's cold outside
leaves blowing all over.

You sat with your coffee and blanket...
Listening to the tinkering of rain
As it hit those big bay windows
surrounding you on all but one side.

Looking out at the big gorgeous oak tree.
Across the way from our low rent
budget friendly fourth floor walkup.

Oh how I remember that run down part of town.

Lost in a daze, I snap out of it
Inhaling the smell of a good read
ready to be devoured by my mind's eye.

Fully entertaining my imagination
This hobby I picked up from you.

Forever remaining thankful.

How many worlds can exist within my own third eye?

(195)

Is this how my brain will always function?
Unable to defog the sadness...

You used to light up the best
most hopeful parts of me.

I used to love my photo collection
memories making me melt.

Now they all just fill me with extreme doubt.

Is love enough?

(121)

Burdened by deceitful commitments.
Anchored in one stale stagnant place.

Shovelled down empty words.
Stripped myself of everything.

Left to bloat, rot and die, all by your design.

Unforgivably, I allow myself to be consumed.

(223)

How can I stay happy?

I must try to relax, as stress washes over me.

I'm drowning in the blue.

(54)

These complex, dulled-out hues of grey
have me seeing shadows.

Each and every single way I look.
I don't know what is real.

Uncertain what is a fictional fragment from my deepest
darkest, weakest moments.

The never-ending black consumes me.

I fade away.

(124)

Dull and void of anything desirable.
An empty shell of a person remains.

Left to wander in hunt of the next.

Constantly struggling.

Desperately searching to fit in.

Never quite belonging anywhere.

(136)

I cannot sleep.
Tossing and turning.
Left to be alone feeling lost inside.

Nightmares make me paranoid.

Paranoia twists me...

...Crinkled into an insomniac mess.

(11)

Take control, feel it and then drop it.
Bury it down low, come on try to forget.

Drowning is no longer an option.

Here comes the blue, sink or swim.

Am I in over my head?

Darkness rushes in
push it back.

Don't look over the edge.
You'll fall through the crack.

Indecisive to go forward, ashes lie behind.
Burned bridges being a coward.

Learn to swim...

I fucking did.

(196)

Struggling to find words to describe how I feel.
The frustration gets to me often mistaken for anger.
Sadness creeps within me, out from the dark.

Grey fog, thick as smoke, fills up my mind.

(177)

I have no care for people that I hurt
those I leave behind.

I no longer feel anything at all.
Choosing to be numb does not mean I am *weak*.

Loving anyone.
Being vulnerable.

Now that is what does.

(174)

My happy fucking birthday...
What a great thing.

Today of all days, left alone
thinking that I'm not special at all.

I wish you would show me how much I mean to you...

...If I mean anything at all.

(107)

I've taken lovers by the dozen.
None come even close.

Thought I met my soulmate
back when I was young.

I knew then
just as I know now.
You're the one I'll want
even after forever.

Waiting along the side lines.

I never understood why.

(239)

Everywhere I look, I see you.

Sometimes just small indications
of your existence inside my world.

Little reminders of the life we had.

Time slipped between our fingers
long before I could stop the flowing.

Occasionally, I am reminded of your glow.

I notice its presence lacking.

I need my own glow.

(70)

Whole body is extremely sore
every inch of me is shaking.
Sweat dripping down my spine
chilling me to my core.

A sickness unlike any other.
Decisions must be made.

Experience this pain, feel it, own it.
Higher and higher
intoxicating myself.

Changing who I am.
Making me tolerable.

Maybe I actually become intolerable?

I'm always so confused.
Days turn into weeks.
Weeks turn into months.
Months turn into years.

Dragging along deep dark lows.
Every sober moment spent thinking of you.

I...
    Don't...
        Want to be...
            Left thinking...
  Of...

                ...Ughhhh...you...

(52)

Pages turn into shots.
Finding myself in a bottle.

Searching through myself.
Flippin' page by page by PAGE.
Not a line in sight that I recognize.

Where did this come from... Who the fuck wrote this?
(Sambuca screams my name.)

(3)

Once or twice before.
Twice back once again.
I've found myself.

> Uh...
> > Uh...
> > > Stumblin'.

Can't see straight, falling on the floor.
Heartbeat racing.

> Just one more.

> > Another kiss.

> > > Another drink.

> Just one more.

> > > Give me another hit.

I can't get enough.
I don't care how rough.

I know it might get tough.
You'll never be enough.

Questioning my right to be obsessive in this love.

Do you feel it, baby?

(158)

Recently I have found
your name is always on the tip of my tongue.

A persistent reminder with heartbreak and pain
an ending too abrupt to share.

My mind sparks alive
dancing with the memories.
Liquored up
soaking in the sorrow...

...Of a lost passion.

(165)

Violent thoughts consume me
pinching at every inch of soft skin.

Memories flood to the surface
of ripping you apart.

I wish to relive them, I love them.

I'm always searching for someone to toss around.

Smack them down
too weak for their own good.

(87)

I tell you things not true
like how nobody else could ever love you.

You will give me all of you.

This is not a choice
I take what I want anyway.

You no longer have a voice
the only option is to surrender.

One way or another
I'll make you do as you're told.

I watch your eyes as they fill with hate.
You'll experience all my wrath.

Soon, your body will be covered in blood.

(57)

Drunker than I thought I'd get.

Hours drinking away all the memories of us together.

Shots of the hard stuff
makes *our* hard stuff...

...A whole lot softer.

(63)

My head is swimming.
I've had too much to drink.

Got me wishing for your presence next to mine.
Forcing me to think...

Oh, how did we go so wrong?

(114)

Times are tough, down low
deep in the rough.

I have nothing to say.
My voice doesn't matter.
I do my best work all alone.

I need more space; I can't breathe.
I want out of this place; it's not safe.
I hate this slow pace; I must keep busy.

Leave me alone!

                        ...Just leave me be...
        ...Wait...
            ...Babe...
                        ...Please...

        ...Don't...go...

I wish I stayed longer; I have so much to say.

Everything I write matters.
Every time, in any place, my voice will be heard.

Luckily, my whole life has been fucking rough.
Way up high or deep down low.

I will forever remain tough.

(85)

I try not to let myself miss your lips pressed to mine.
Desperate to experience your most passionate kiss.

Instead, I'll turn to my oldest vice
rip myself open, slice my skin.

The blade slices
releasing all emotion as we know them.

This pain numbs me, grants me freedom.
Watch as I bleed, draining out empathy.

Breathe in...

...Tranquility.

(169)

There is no winning
my disease wants me dead.

Why should I keep fighting?

This war, it's all in my head.
Battling only myself.

The more I fight
the weaker I become.

At least that's how I feel.
Always knew I was dumb.

Alcohol makes me real.

Without it...
            ...I cannot be...

                    ...Numb.

(185)

All I want for Christmas is blood, pills, pain, and booze.

All I want is to see the other side.
Tired of feeling trapped, nowhere to turn.
Unable to run, take this feeling.

Make it go away.

(215)

Even when I'm not alone, I still feel it.
Loneliness creeps up.

I don't need it.

(99)

Here we go again
this vicious pattern.

A sick and twisted cycle.

Always coming around.
Leaving almost too quickly.
Never staying in one place.

A wisp of air.
Grasping for light.
Unable to feel.
Unable to touch.

Constantly a brightly moving blur.

Let me in.
Allow me to get close
so I can poison your thoughts.

Embrace me tighter
while I'm trying to weaken your mentality.

If you love me
I'll destroy your very being.

(88)

Far-fetched fantasies
dazed off and days away.

Never quite reaching
everything I ever dreamed for.

Achievement forever unseen.

On the horizon ahead?
Nothing but gloom foreseen.

(172)

Self-harm helps
however temporary it may be.
It brings me back out of the darkest of places.

I know there's one thing
which always makes everything "A-OK."

First, I've got to get a hold of something
so long as it can break through my skin.

Cause the bleeding to begin.

(125)

A numbing, tingling sort of pain.
Desperate to feel anything.

I pinch my skin, and nothing happens.
Punching myself results in a tickle.
Burns cause only a slight pain.

The real endorphins come from cutting.
Watching the blood drip down my wrist onto my thigh.

Now that's what I call...

...A fucking suicide high.

(178)

I can honestly say nothing in life will ever go your way.
Hold on tight, remember to pray.

If you get lucky you'll die without pain.

(208)

How can I be fine and then not?

One second unstoppable
then everything is crumbling.

How do I hold myself together?

I don't wanna be like this forever.

(118)

Struggling is what I do best.
Fighting constantly with who I am.
Caught between want and need.

Lying to myself
feeding my own enemy.

Destruction of my life.
Weak in the knees for a bottle.

Mentally dependent on wasting away.
Absolutely incapable of change.

-      A genuine description of me.

(131)

I saw the light dim in her eyes
only then did I let go of her neck.

Hands tightly pressing in
I watched her struggle for air.
Silently pleading for me to let go.

Can't remember what got us there.

The screaming, the nagging
her annoying fucking breathing?

I took her to the brink of death
enjoying every last moment of it.

Guaranteed I won't forget that.

I brought her back and kept her alive.
What a rush it really is.
Playing God, with someone's life at risk.

How lucky she must've felt
sleeping with a monster in her bed.

(76)

Missing something that is not mine to miss.
Feelin' like a fraud inside my own life.

Gotta figure it out one way or another
who I really am deep down inside.

I won't like what I see.
I cannot allow myself to give in and feel.

What has already been stolen.
What continues to give so freely.

A piece of me to share with everyone
anyone wanting to touch.

Caress me, fuck me, kiss me anywhere.

One condition: ~~do not fall in love with me.~~
                            do not show me love.

(108)

Often consider myself a "we."

Deep within my subconscious
resting, waiting, anticipating attention.

A secondary persona resides
actively trying to take control.

Any slight slip up, the tiniest mistake
would result in my fate.

Every movement
constantly being judged.
Worried for my time in this world
could fall into the black.

Replaced by some impersonation.
Some fake carbon cut-out
a plastic copy of me
roaming around living my life.

Am I losing my mind?

(129)

Yearning for satisfaction, failing to find my niche.

Looking for the place I belong.
Searching for far too long.
Learning constantly along the way.

Maybe I just don't fit in.

(116)

Feeling stuck.
Trapped within.

Tapped of all energy to fight.
Hopelessly afraid.

I may have lost my mind...

Who would even care, right?

134)

Overwhelmed with thoughts of breaking
every single thing I own.

However, I know that's irrational.

I would regret that immediately.
That's one tape I'm able to play through.

Instead, I hit myself.

No longer punching walls.
No more smashing things.

Instead, I'll give myself a fat lip.

Less than nine punches to bruise me.

(123)

Struggling to live a little more.
Attempting to experience the excitement in living life.

Deep down
I feel nothing.

Fixated on the adrenaline pumping.
Embracing the wind in my hair.

Finally, I've decided.

I no longer care.
My brains might just end up all over your floor.

(176)

I'm on a path that leads nowhere.

All I leave behind is destruction.
Hoping to take myself down deeper as I go.
It may not happen quickly.

However, it will be done.

(175)

How long does death wait for someone's life to end?

So, why not take the ones who are *begging* to go
those *praying* to die?

If death were less patient
maybe then we would know why.

(86)

A craving deep inside.
Urgently wearing down my will.
Set free this life within me.

The dance of a razor
gliding through this external shell holding me here.

Searching for spirituality.
My soul aches to be released back into the universe
to exist among the cosmos.

Terminally unique
yet all the same.

When the time comes, I promise to accept the flat
line.

Fuck everything, will this be life or death?

(84)

Dig a fucking grave.
It's official; my time is up.

I can no longer be brave.

(132)

How not to hurt myself:

Tell someone...
...Just *tell* someone.

Reach out to people.
Shouldn't it be that easy?

Just tell *anyone...*
...I'm ready to take a knife to my skin.

Just say the words...
...*I need help.*

But I can't...
I just can't.

I cannot force these words to come out.
I want someone to come running to my side.
Maybe even rescue me.

But...

My pain wants another thing.
To cut into myself.

See myself bleed, slowly a few drips come to surface.
Get brave, go deep enough
soon, a steady flow of red will pour.

You cannot hurt me when I hurt myself.

(199)

If I fucked off
everyone would be happier.

Changing myself to please
the effort has become too much.

Trying to create a new me
I've been awful for so long.

Finding difficulty loving myself
just easier to end it all.

(240)

Responsibility suffocates me
it's a part of growing up.

That's what I've always been told.

Each day slowly
tightening around my neck.

Getting closer and closer to death.

Why grow old?
I want to live forever.

(156)

Two halves don't make a whole.

One side of me feels empty.
Incomplete and incapable.
Always finding the line.
Failing to push further or harder.

The other is full of motivation.
Willing, spiritual and free.
Always striving and searching
for something more, anything better.

How can these opposites exist within the same place?

Constant bloodshed
pulling, tearing, and splitting my psyche into two.
Rip my heart from my chest.

Life is a painful existence.

(161)

Afraid of failure.
Terrified of my own shadow.

Each step took with thoughtful doubt.
Over analyzing all circumstances.

Hypothetical situations
have me standing in a puddle of nervous sweat.

Unrealistic occurrences tearing me apart.

(89)

The way I live is rough.
Taking whatever is available.

Life is all about the give and take.

In the blink of an eye
you can have everything
without realizing it means nothing.

All you know could be snatched away.
No warning to be had
zero signs to alert.

Unaware of the dangers to living life.

Without a care in the world.

(79)

Aware of the tiredness taking over.
Every bone in my body aches.

How can I feel so old when I've hardly lived at all?
Wisdom beyond my years is what was always said.

All those extra days catching up to me.
I feel them as if they were real.

(73)

I always believed my mind was a bore.

Years spent playing sports
nothing else was expected.
Well at least not much more.

Only I knew of the world inside my head.

Fields of purple grass
fuzzy and tall.
Yellow clouds blowing across beautiful green skies.
The bright blue sun shining down across my land.

I kept all that locked away.

Enemies of mine turn into beasts and horror goblins.
Family and friends become whimsical towns folk
all with adventurous lives.

Those who burn deep inside my soul I've discovered
are majestic-type monarchs
waiting to be found along the way.

Each journey is different from the last.
Love making, dragon taming
discovering new land, and surviving by my own hand.

The quest of my life.
Nobody sees... Nobody knows.

This is the place where
I'm the only one who ever goes.

(102)

A dragon or some sort of beast.
Scaly, prickly
possibly toxic on all sides.

Yeah, that's basically me.
Stopped denying
anything too close is slowly dying.

Embracing this life now.

Discarding damaged bones
roughly six feet behind me.

Trinkets like reminders kept
memories to ponder fondly.

Just once I might look back to recall who I used to be.

(126)

Stopping to smell the roses?
More like halting because of the bullshit.

Life is nothing but a string of strange
or awkward situations.

Every once in a while...
Remember to evaluate it all.

(43)

A flashback overcomes me:
Everything happened so quickly.
One minute
happy in recovery...

        ...The next, I'm piss drunk.
Seeing red with rage.

    ...Directed...
        ...Only at you.

We promised, no matter what happened.
Love would remain between us.
Little did I know
I was being manipulated.

See you'd been drinking behind my back.
Spinning web after web of lies.
I had no idea I was under attack.
My sobriety out the window.

With nothing left to lose
I threw punches.
Left deep dark marks all over...
you...

    ...Screaming... begging...
        ...Clawing at me...

    ...Desperately hoping I would stop...

(186)

Attempting to understand my strange desire.

To pick things from the past.
Favour them all over again.

If it didn't work once
why think it will now?

Nothing has changed.
Still the same old me.

(244)

This never-ending, toxic-fucking cycle.
Follows me everywhere I go.

Every move I make, *wrong.*
Leading me back around.

Which next step could be the right one?
Too many possibilities, afraid to continue this...

... Absolute insanity.

(170)

Each road ahead
leads me to the same damn intersection.

A four-way stop between...

Life spent slowly dying and miserable.
A desperately sad and painful demise.
My messy expiration as an alcoholic.

          Or

The last path that I could take
would lead me to a comfortable way out
old and in my own loving bed.

Whichever direction I go...

          ...There is no surviving...

...Me.

(258)

Let it go.

It could benefit someone else.

(167)

Fuck, I want to die.

I want to travel back in time
change the things I've done.
Go back to where it all went wrong.

Too many heart aches, so much pain.
Avoidable, given just one trip...

...Back in time

Lend me a DeLorean
or bring me The Doctor in the Tardis.

I'm ready to start over without the hard work.
Take me back to those early days.

When I was still... growing.

I want to go back to when I was young.
Back before things got too messy.
When I had a choice
a chance to be who I was meant to be.

Regardless
it is too late and there is no going back.

The only way to change...do the damn work.

(95)

I've always been the flight over fight type of person.

I would run so fast
in any direction.
Rather than stay. facing up to how I feel.

Forever the heartbreaker
yet always heartbroken.

I've run from you before.

Experienced a familiar feeling.
Didn't quite understand.
I'm stopping, standing still.

This time I'm choosing to fight.

NEW LIFE
NEW FEARS

(71)

Embracing the breaking of our bond.

Embarking on this adventure
that is, being alone to fend for myself.

Knowing full well
independence was never our issue.

You never noticed the fragile bits
falling all over the place as I crumbled.

Now I'm nothing more than a pile of ash
gathered perfectly at your feet.
Charred to coal.

My body, constantly smouldering
just barely burning
somehow still connected to the flame inside of you.

Hoping the day will come
when that passion reignites in favour of me.

A Phoenix will rise.

This cold hell that is my being
will emerge into something worth loving.

(221)

How can I take back a feeling
or an experience
without changing who I am?

I don't write to hurt anyone.
Only to write out the hurt within me...

(44)

I bought an empty book made with beautiful leather bound with a drawstring.

I hoped it would instill inspiration.

It left me as blank as its pages.

(117)

"I just want you back."
I write those words and I feel like a fraud.

I know how I feel.
I'm afraid I've always known.

Loving you, well—
That's a waste of time.

(225)

Will you see the poser in me?

Always giving one face to the world.
A mask for all to see.

When, really, that person isn't me.

(122)

I want to believe love exists.
Feel it everywhere
see it in everything.

Remaining only a blank empty space.
Void of everything.
Without passion.

Our chance of survival?
Slimming constantly.

Actions lose all meaning.

(220)

Opening up can be so scary.

Showing people a secret side is a vulnerability
often mistaken for weakness.

(78)

Never have I met someone so damn divine.
I find myself thinking of you all the time.

Deep down, you know it's true
the way you move your body is so damn fine.

You excite me in a very specific way
like the way one would feel surrounded by landmines.

(59)

Since my lips were graced by your name
certain routine phrases
coined sayings tossed around...
Have ever since changed meaning.

I've always been passionate
I will forever be intense.

You're the spark that lights my flame
the fuel to my burning fire.

I would gladly be engulfed by this love.

(46)

When I think of your hands
I feel weak all over.
When I imagine your lips on me
from deep within I begin to quiver.

When I dream of your eyes
I am once again left completely vulnerable to you.

(8)

Your eyes on me smile so fucking bright.

I can't help this feeling, *fuck it*
I won't even fight.
I would say I'm falling
although we are so far past that.

I can always hear you calling.
I've been hooked ever since that first night we met.

Chasing after your heart–how I want it to be mine.

For nights now
I've dreamt of this.

In front of me you look so damn fine.
I'm marvelled by your beauty
in shock over your wisdom.

You remain cool like it's your duty.

Do you even feel this, like I do?

(180)

Imagine this...

Slipping myself deep inside of you
I feel how wet you are.
With a quick look between us
a burst of desire ripples through.

Picturing myself bending you over
the chair, table, or the bed.

Please let me show you just how much I love you.

With a quick crack
my knuckles slide inside you.
Not gentle, not rough either.

This is what we both needed.

In these moments
I connect deeply to you.
Our bodies rock together
Closer...
            ...Closer, until we become one.

(164)

They're made of magic whenever they show up.
My mind takes a deep dive.
Lust in full swoon.

They make my heart beat thrice as fast.
Nervous that our love will never last.

You're already spoken for.

(139)

"You are the person I probably would
have ended up with if I didn't get married."

-       The worst words to hear from the lips
of the person you love most in this world.

(245)

Sitting around obsessing
over someone or something...

...So long, so far gone.

...Is the true waste of time.

(202)

Don't want to let you down
pushing myself every day.

Won't let you see me drown.

(218)

The curve of your body when you lean into me...
Like two puzzle pieces.

I swear I had never fit anywhere before your arms.

When the smell of you fills my nose...

   ...I know I had never smelled anything so sweet.

(229)

The way they sleep
so soft, like an angel.

I swear I've never seen someone so fair.
Innocence exuberant from their skin.

With each breath they take
I fall more and more in love.

When I'm in their arms
I'm on top of the world.

Nothing and nobody can stop this love.

(219)

My love for you...

Is it returned to me the same?
Or of an equal desire?

I know you say our love is true.
Do you promise you feel it too?

(203)

Attempting to express...

           ...My deep desire...

                  ...To be deep

...Inside of you.

(179)

I crave intimacy in-between the sheets.
A constant struggle
two opposing ideals.

Could I find one person to love forever?
            Or take new lovers as often as possible?

The exciting feeling of new hands
a body yet to be discovered.
Passion coursing through veins.
I can't find this feeling in just one person.

Always loved being in love
the comfort of a significant other.
Safely falling asleep with one another
waking up to their arms around me.

I want both passion and comfort.
Can I find that in you?

(6)

Holding it down.
Trying to bury away my thoughts and feelings.
Knowing damn well you'd take it too far.

If I let on how you make my heart race
with the anticipation of your touch...
Would you comfort me?
Could I spend forever in your eyes?

I can't stay
or I know I'll have to say, "Fuck it all."
I'll spill the beans
confess to you, my deepest secrets.

How I'd love to see your face twist
watch the smile creep up to your lips.
You'd know you'd be in control
would you say it's still the same?

Would you spit in my face?
(I'm begging you, please.)

(25)

Don't say a word. *(remind yourself)*
Just keep your mouth shut
giving a reaction is your choice.

Keep that power
own it for yourself.
You don't owe it to anybody.

They say things to get a rise. *(playfully)*
Their motivation is your destruction
think ahead and tread carefully.

A pattern of bad behaviour followed
creeping in, urging me to make a move.
I can stop it...
...I can't stop it.

Little slips along the way
overall change is progress.
Forgive yourself for feeling weak
vulnerability allows for growth.

You're stronger than you feel in this moment
when you're feeling your weakest.

(9)

Countdown begins, my time to win.
Lost the last time around.
I won't let that happen again.

Adrenaline pumping, anxiety is thumping.
Heart beating, palms begin to sweat...

You remain so chill, calm as can be.
While I'm losing my cool, is this how it's going to be?

So be it, I just wanna have sex with you.
Take control, take me now.
Winning isn't everything, looks like I've lost again.

I've gained more from this than you'll know.

(182)

I want to go there now, my place of escape.
I crave the feeling of you *cumming* undone
all over my fingers.

I desire to be deep inside you.

(140)

They say they like their people hard on the outside
soft on the inside.
I've never felt a more perfect description
for who I am as a person.

They need a body to warm
my icy cold hands wishing always to be just that.
If you're craving a cool loving touch
to simmer your raging core.

Look no further. I'm right here.

(233)

They cleared away all the cobwebs.
The ones I allowed to gather over time.

To fill the deepest, darkest places of me.

Examined all the bad behaviour.
Looked me in the eyes, pierced me when they told
me...

They still love me, accept me.
Will help me find the strength within...

To light those dark corners and continue to grow.

(19)

Sometimes I think I'll regret this decision.
This change of life is so drastic.

From time to time, I wonder when
you'll come crawling back.

I want you to know that if you do
I won't be here waiting for you.

I've found someone else.

I know they will love me fiercely.
With more passion than you ever exhibited.

Your whole body won't miss me.
Your heart won't ever ache.
Longing for my touch won't stress your heart.

You may grow weary...
Do best to remember we grew apart.

(157)

I think we both know, I'm ready for this.
Found the way to love you properly.
You showed me the way to your heart.

You're the person I love the most
the one I see my future with.
You make me weak in the knees
breaking down all my walls.

Can't help but worry that I won't ever be enough.
Regardless, I'll never stop trying
to show you how worthy I am.

Working hard always to prove,
I can be what you need.

The love of my life, you mean everything to me.

(5)

Your hand in mine
we both know where this leads.

Your head on my chest
we both know what this means.
Your hand caressing my hips
we both know what we need.

Racing upstairs
cannot contain this much longer
Sparks ignite between us
leave us aching for more.

A burning passion inside me
taking your clothes off, you can't help yourself.

Tasting every inch of my flesh
as I'm slowly becoming more exposed.

I can see your excitement growing.
Pupils dilate, telling me you're ready.
I can't help but enjoy every second
bringing you closer and closer.

You're feeling me all over you
letting out soft gasps of pleasure.
Exploring new territory together
I'll make tonight unforgettable.

I want us to last.

(10)

I wasn't looking for this...

I just wanted a play toy.

...A body to touch.

Someone to fuck.

Already thinking you'd found love
the person you hoped will last a lifetime.

To my surprise, they became the first person
to make *fucking* seem so different.

Something sensual and unforgettable.
An experience unlike any other
a craving beyond my regular appetite.

Should have known when I'm least expecting
you'd strike my guard down.

I've never made love with anyone.
...Other than you.

(53)

We love so intensely; I know it's meant to be.
No matter where I go, you're all I ever see.

Their temperature is rising
while they are constantly romanticizing.

Me and them mutually climaxing...
We touch, we kiss, our bodies rub together.

Sparks fly like the first of July.

(222)

I know what we have can be so beautiful.
We just have to let ourselves be happy.

(80)

Feeling me up...

Your hands all over my body...

Mind is swimming...

Unable to focus...

Count with me...

One...deep breath in...

Two...exhale everything...

Three...take a moment...

Four...don't lose yourself...

You want me baby, and you know I want you too.

(235)

I crave to feel their wetness up against me.
They're always ready when I need them to be.

I want to take them places
we've both never been before.

They're willing to try exciting new things.

When we cum together...
          ...It's always a good time.

(226.2)

Can they care for me?
Will they nurture my soul?
When I'm sick, would they make the right soup?
Coerce me into a warm bath?

Will I be let down again?

(36)

To walk away or trudge through the trenches?
Unknowingly plagued with uncertainty.
Thick like mud, dragging you down.

Fog rolls in, darkened by despair.
Two steps forward, one back.

Scared of what the night brings.

Face the battle head on.
Sacrifice a piece of who you are.
Turning away would be cowardice.

Either way, the only one to save you
has to be you.

(228)

When you find something special, hold on tight.

Is this real love?
Stay and fight.

This is your time to embrace love and make it right.

I want this to last.

(198)

Memories flood to the surface.
I find myself questioning my worth.

How can I deserve love?

I've hurt all those who dare get close to my heart
for as long as I remember.

(201)

What is this?
All I want is to be free.

(206)

Desire to have more than one lover.
Wanting to have all my needs met.

Someone is always there for me
helping me however I need.
Supporting me, caring for my mental health.

One lover, to fit each need.
The more the merrier, especially in my loving bed.

(7)

Could you live with just a piece of me?
Would you still love me the same?
If you had to share my body with other people too…?

Understand that my soul belongs to you
in a way I don't yet understand.

I wish to learn; I want to grow beside you hand in
hand.
This need inside me flares; the flames creep up inside.

For many years I tried and tried.
My secrets
I felt a need to hide.

Desire for a taste on the wild side.
Loving deeply, free as I please
new lovers between my sheets.

This part of me is missing, I cannot hide anymore.

(144)

I wanted to portray
the picture-perfect version of my life.
Presenting so prim and proper.

The perfect lie, told to everyone, even myself.

My intentions are crystal clear
with only recovery on my mind.

Leaving out the dark truth
purposely avoiding anything real.

No longer will I hide
behind this carefully created facade.

(152)

I keep hoping you'll show up, knock on my door
missing me, wanting kisses, desiring to be touched.

I keep trying to shake this
wondering, am I going to make it?

I would hold you through any struggle
try hard to make you laugh.
Anything to comfort you.
Wishing you would come by my house.

It's a safe place for you
always and forever will be.
Lying here, waiting.
I want to know you're safe
I'm desperate for you to be happy.

I stay awake hoping to hear from you.
You asked for a break, no contact for nine days.

First day of absolutely no contact...
I miss you more than ever.

How can I sleep when you're not next to me?
Do I dare close my eyes, to then dream of you?

I'll always be here, especially when you need me.

I want you to need me.
Please come over.

Begging the universe for you to stop by.

(149)

I have to be up wicked early
yet I lie here wide awake.

My mind won't stop racing
preventing the drift from taking me away.
Not focusing on stress
kept awake only by my desire for you to show up.

My entire nervous system
is brightly ablaze, on fire for you.

Every nerve ending sparked alive with your touch.

(254.2)

I know you need distance, more so than I do.

Now why can't you see I agree...

That's just not for me.

When you're not around
I'm left to question my sanity.
Happier than ever before
yet I struggle to see.

Why is it I hate being left all alone with myself
actively ignoring my darkest places?

(147)

Please show up
come knock on my door.
Plead for me to hold you.
Request all of the kisses.

I would give everything just to be next to you.
I will endure any painful moment.

Come cry with me.
Show up just to lie next to me.

Find myself wanting to call.
Constantly thinking of your voice.

How can I change my thinking?

(247)

I can't let go.
I will try, though.

Rarely ever does "I have to"
feel like "I want to."

This time, "I have to" is the only choice.

And...
...I don't want to.

(151)

My hobbies include hanging at home, sitting on my
couch vaping.
Likely I'll tell you that I read, I write, or maybe even
about time with my pet snake.

What I won't tell you, one thing I won't ever mention...
Sometimes, I'll open my previous partner's Facebook
account.

Luckily, still logged in.

I watch their conversations, activities.
I scheme ways to get them back.

I will never tell you this.

You may wonder why.
I want you to think I'm healthy, that I'm recovered.
A strong independent.

I'll say anything, because all I really want to do
is sleep with you.
Get into your pants as fast as I can.

Help myself to a fix of BDSM.
Before you see the real me.

(153)

My toxic trail.

I allow myself to engage in unhealthy behaviour.
Just enough to stay sick.
So long as I can convince myself...

Well, *"at least I'm not drinking."*
I'm healthy and I'm doing *"better."*
"I deserve a little fun."

Lead her on, pretending to show interest.
Making sure to show
only what I deemed useful to my cause.

Lied about work life
kept secrets to myself.
Act like some big shot
puffing myself up enough.

I act the way I knew would be of optimal interest.
Allowing me to manipulate.
Using you.

After the fact
I'm still broken.
I'm still not who I want to be.

All I know how to do is drop you.

I see in the aftermath how many I've hurt.
My eyes are open to the mess I made.
The worst part of me is still running my life.

(237)

Right when I thought I put myself where I belong
I moved my life onto a path I thought was for me.

So why is it, after everything, I feel so lost?

(154)

My mind escapes me
searching for answers.
Diving deep within
I look for myself.

Wondering about *who* I could be.
Confused as to where I stand.
What will I be a year from now?

The possibilities are endless.
Many options lie just ahead.
Unable to know which is best.

Getting lost in thought, losing all sense of oneself.

Swirling deeper
spiralling downwards.
Desperate for an escape.
Looking at old vices.

Patterns and behaviours that once saved me
now might see me to my death.

(246)

Seeing these patterns.
Recognizing this cycle.

One step forward to discovering the real me.

(148)

I know my obsession is codependency
soaked in alcoholism.

I know this pain is where my alcoholic self resides.
Doing full-on pushups
waiting patiently.

Building itself up
eager to take me down.
Still, I sit here and obsessively contemplate
hoping for you to just show up.

Anticipating your knock at my door.

I want you so badly, I love you even more.

(142)

Aware of self-growth
feels sorta like having my personal security blanket
yanked away and I'm fighting.

Aspects of my character deemed to be "inadequate."

Without those personality traits
the ones I've relied on for far too long.

What will be left of me?

(166)

Without the drinking, the using
lying, or the manipulation...

How can I continue to be me?

I don't know who I am.

(133)

A burden, the great void inside myself.
I cannot seem to find a way to hide.
I must face this feeling.

(197)

I've done so many wrong things.
Always the one to make bad decisions.
Walking along such a strange path.
Was this meant for me?

Am I strong enough to hold this weight?

(21)

Everything inside is broken.
A million pieces lay below.

I tried to pick them up to
put them back together.
In a frenzy to mend things
I used glue and sticky gum.

Panicking to make things right
I attempted to seal the cracks.

Scotch and packing tape.
Failed to fill the gaps with glue.
Only after failure did I realize...

Some things can never be fixed.

Once I could see that
everything started coming together.

Is this just a delusion?

(230)

I don't want to be afraid anymore.
Forever jumping at my own shadow.
Constantly looking over my shoulder.
A paranoid android expecting the worst.

How can I anticipate good things...
When I can't even trust my own thinking or
behaviour?

A collection of past patterns is emerging
taking me down.

I just want to feel whole.

(253)

You are my home
even while I'm away.
Finding my way back
no matter how far I've strayed.

Your arms, my safe place being held by you.
I become one again, refilled, and grounded.

The life of freedom is the life for me.
Able to express myself
by following every whim.

Comfortably knowing my home life
is capable of going on without me.

Waiting to embrace me once again.

(62)

I had a moment tonight...
Close to a relapse but without action.

A blade through my skin was what I desired.

Instead, I just let myself scream your name.

(51)

Listen to love.

When they say it's okay, they mean it.
When they ask you not to do something
respect that.

When they present to you their soul
tell them how beautiful it is.

When they give you their heart...
Carry it, treasure it
wear it like the badge of honour it is.

(130)

Choke me tight, slice me up, I'm nothing
just a piece of meat.

I love to do as I'm told.
If I disobey you
I want to be beat.

In the specific mood for receiving punishment
it's too easy to get what I want.

Pretending not to hear the command given
for me to wait, cumming anyways, I like to taunt.

Flip me over to smack my ass, wanting more.
I'll beg and plead, dripping at the lips, anticipating.

Fucking pound me.

Please, hit me until I bleed.

(252)

What I do now will affect who I become.
To go on and ultimately shape this
fragile future that we hold in our hands now.

If I continue slipping, I'll keep on fumbling.
Only then our fate will surely be set.

(104)

I can see myself running, sweating
all red and huffing.

Towards a great unknown
unlikely I make it there alive.

I promised I'd work hard.
Never giving up, can't show my bluff.

Giving everything I have ensured my survival.

(251)

The first thing I had to do was admit ineffectiveness.

Found myself weakened
worn down by years of use
wasted away with substance abuse.

Half of my problem
was I felt completely in control of everything.
I could persuade and manipulate
the pants off anyone without issue.

Take you with my own hands
mould you into my ideal perfect person.

Made exactly to suit only my needs.

(90)

Weak and vulnerable, I gave my will over
to do as I'm told, following every order.

You are so passionate, treating me like royalty.
Spanking me, only when I've earned it.

I'm glad we were able to agree
it pleases you to watch me...
          ...On my knees begging
            "please."

It's an honour to serve you.
Living my best life, under your foot.

(209)

I love you x infinity

I love you, I accept every part of you.
I love you, regardless of the bullshit.

I love you, even for what you've been through.
I love you, especially when things get tough.
I love you desperately when I'm being rough.
I love you when your eyes pierce my soul.

I love you, excited feeling you in my arms.
I love you for always supporting me.
I love you when you try to level me.
I love you for all the experiences that shaped you.

I love you more than the air I breathe.
I love you for motivating me to be better.
I love you, thanks for accepting the worst of me.

(243)

I can still feel this excitement.
Statically charged and surging with each pulse.
Undeniably powerful, passionate love making.

It's brand new and oh, so electrifying.
I guess I've always been a sucker for punishment.
Grateful to have finally found a healthy outlet.

(23)

All I needed was some coffee.

Clarity and certainty.
Offering itself to me.
Freedom screaming.
Flying towards me.
Everything falling into place.
Everlasting love for you.

Cream and sugar.

(162)

One step after the other, inch by inch.
I continue to grow.

We each follow separate pathways.
Leading us to where we belong.
Learning as we go.

Open your mind, take in life with a positive attitude.

Love what you do, be who you are.

Won't let anyone else decide my damn fate.

(143)

Growth is a strange thing.
Sometimes it's subtle, sometimes glaringly obvious.

Having lived protected by all my bad behaviours for
years and years, sometimes I'm not sure how to act,
or respond to situations.

Luckily with growing, things start to clear up.

Instinct shows me the way.

I had to spend a long time reflecting.
Really digging into myself to figure out each of those
defective characteristics of my personality.

I will stare them in the face
fight every urge to act on them.

Slowly, I start to see myself transform.

(141)

Life in sobriety is hard enough
without having to find oneself.

That is all it is, though.
Destroying the old me.
My old way of thinking, reconstructing
into a "happier, healthier" person.

Building with the pebbles and the pieces
left behind from the wreckage of my past.

Show me what's real
please teach me how to feel.
Find that fine line between the overreaction
or a genuine one.
Finding a deeper connection
with a consciousness greater than mine.

How to find a life that fits these strict, ideal
directions?

Whatever that might even mean...

Keep in mind the rusty, day old quotes like
          "You're not alone."

Except I am.

Friends and family
begin to feel more like acquaintances.

Nights spent alone, days pass by
without a single inquiry into how I'm surviving.
I find myself all alone
the only one with all this work to do, struggling.

Figuring myself out.
Relying on something much different than I'm used to
to guide me in the right direction.

(145)

Going into the new year
feeling like a whole new me.

A sober human filled with hope.
Equally filled with fear.

Will I continue along this path?
I know just what I need to do.
Thorough and rigorous perseverance.
Two traits I am not too familiar with.

Continuing the hard work
learning how to be
the best version of myself that I can be.

A me that is respectful, loving, and kind
with aspiration to care and be loyal.

With the chance to really dig deep
I'll continue to blossom into the real me.

(128)

My future has not yet been determined.
Not by anything or by anyone, especially not my past.

Who I can become.
What I might accomplish.

That's only up to me.

(238)

The time that I have left feels like a prison sentence.
Trapped inside these four walls.
Unable to seek change or the freedom I desire.

I must maintain my mental state.
Too easily, I could fall into insanity.

Holding myself together.
Just a little...longer.

Once this is over, I'll have the world again.

(127)

Two months passed...
I couldn't see myself.

Blurred between lines...
Who I used to be.

Three more months gone by.
One would hardly believe...
This mess of a person, to actually be me.

A drunken haze of confusion...
Starting to see doubles.

Six months ago...
I didn't know where to turn.
Would never have given this a second thought.

Today...
I think, maybe I do have a future.
I can be more than just my past...

(254.3)

You know I need distance, more so than you do.
However, we always find a way to agree.

Now we both spend quality time alone, happily.
Occasional downtime separately spent
with friends, doing an activity, or just hanging out.

Benefiting our relationship and is very rewarding
I love my time, now more than ever before.

Compromise is truly a gift.

(214)

What matters most
is not about who has made you cum
or who was the most fun.

What matters most— that we respect one another.
Also we're still happy together.

Me and you, exploring ourselves freely.
Sometimes with others
nothing else can compare.

Focusing mainly on our love
all about the freedom to be our individual selves.

(189)

I wanted to write a book
to prove that my love for you was so strong.

Turns out I needed to write to learn what I need.

More importantly...

        ...How to fucking love me.

ABOUT THE AUTHOR

Vex LaBoucane (They/Them/Theirs)

Vex is a Canadian born poet with personal experience in mental illness, abuse, and addiction. This book has been years in the making, chronicling the stages of some of their darkest experiences. They are passionate about nature, family, friends, and healing as they continue on their journey of recovery.

9 780228 853428